Surviving Addiction,
ONE DAY AT A TIME

TY HOWELL

PAGE PUBLISHING
Conneaut Lake, PA

First originally published by Page Publishing 2024

ISBN 979-8-89315-140-4 (pbk)
ISBN 979-8-89315-153-4 (digital)

Printed in the United States of America

Acknowledgments

Thank you for supporting me.

I would like to thank the recovery groups and people who have helped me and supported me along the way of my journey. First and foremost, my amazing family for never giving up on me through all the hard years and setbacks. Without them, I'd be nowhere, and possibly homeless.

I would like to thank my sponsor; he has never given up on me since my first rehab. He answers my calls and calls me out on my stupidity. He also took me to my first AA meeting. He's a straight shooter, and I need that.

Aware Recovery, they have been with me for almost a year now, even when I was relapsing all the time. When I was giving up on myself, they picked me back up and got me the help I needed. They come to me and make it extremely easy to connect with. They are an amazing company. I am going to be sad to see them go.

And to anyone else I've met along the way who gave me support or just reached out to see how I was doing. All that stuff matters when dealing with this disease. But for everyone I've listed, I honestly couldn't have done it without them. And I just wanted to say thank you from the bottom of my heart!

Introduction

My name is Ty Howell, and yes, I am an addict. I am currently in short-term recovery. And God willing, I will make it to long-term recovery. Recovery is a full-time job itself, and the work is never over—ever! I would love to do anything to help myself escape the reality of the real world. That meant for me taking painkillers, smoking weed, drinking, and doing kratom. If I couldn't find that, I would do whatever I could get my hands on. That meant cocaine, Suboxone. I was not afraid to travel to find it, no matter where it took me or who I had to deal with. It was a job! Sometimes an all-day job at that. My brain was and still can be my own prison. I felt since I wasn't putting a needle in my arm, it was okay. This has been a journey for me that I am still on. It continues to test my strength and character. I've had self-pity and setbacks, but so far, I have grown through them to have a better understanding of myself and this disease.

Addiction, in my own words, is simple. It takes everything you love and slowly rips it away from you—family, friends, relationships, money, and self-respect. It leaves you wondering, Why is this happening to me? I came from a great family. I knew better. I was raised better than this. Both parents had amazing jobs. Mom was a registered nurse, and my father worked for a Fortune 500 company. Both had very respectable jobs. My brother, who lived with us, was a hard worker who provided well for his family. I didn't think I had a problem. I didn't see it. I didn't lose anything; I gave it away to this disease. If left untreated, it can and will get worse. It's progressive, which means it gets worse over time. Drug addiction can be a big stigma; that's why drug addicts use and use until it's too late and they cross that imaginary line, in which after that, it's too late. There's no going back! But it is possible to break this stigma and recover! How do I know this, you may ask? Because it happened to me, it got so bad for me I had to find the strength to say something and get help. It was a very long journey full of misery. My name is Ty Howell, and this is my story…

Chapter 1

Early Childhood

Growing up, I had a great childhood. My parents took me and my brother skiing, swimming, camping trips, and on a trip to Disney World. We also spent summer vacations at our grandparents' condo in Marco Island, Florida. My brother and I grew up in a small town in Ohio. We were actually considered a village with one stoplight. There wasn't much to do unless you traveled thirty minutes to an hour away. So you could say life was somewhat boring unless you played sports in school or tried to find something to do. Growing up, my brother and I never got along until we were older. I always felt like the black sheep of the family. My brother and I got away with things we probably should not have. We had rules in our house that we had to abide by. However, there were those times when nobody knew what we were doing. We lived on a dead-end street that had a field behind us. Our neighborhood was full of kids. My parents' house was the place we all would end up at.

I would say eighth grade was when I drank alcohol for the first time. My friends and I were camping and got ahold of some Jameson with a chaser of Mountain Dew. Christ, it was horrible, but it got the job done. My two friends and I, we don't talk much anymore, because in my addiction days, I alienated myself. But that night, we got pretty drunk. I remember that warm feeling hitting me pretty hard, that feeling of relaxation and euphoria hitting you hard. It felt amazing. We were laughing, stumbling, falling down, just being dumb kids. I always felt shy and somewhat out of place, but I would always hide it from friends and family. But when I first took that drink, my shyness melted away. And I loved that feeling. I knew I wanted to do that again. My grandparents lived not too far away from me. My grandpa had his own liquor cabinet in the basement. Once in a while, I would go over there, and when I could, I would take their small Gatorade bottles and fill them up with his whiskey. I had them hidden behind his bar. When I had a chance, I would sneak them over to my parents' house. That worked out for the longest time. Lucky me, I never got caught. I didn't drink every day, but if there was a chance I could get away with it, you bet your ass I was going to shoot down some whiskey to get that feeling back again. I'm pretty sure no one knew about it.

Also, in school, I was a wrestler and played a little football. I wasn't the best; my brother was. I was good enough to make varsity. I wrestled from first grade until I graduated high school. I hated being in front of crowds. Wrestling gave me so much anxiety I almost quit. But my dad was really good at sports, and my brother was amazing; I didn't want to let them down. So I stuffed my emotions deep down inside myself and stuck it out. Every day, my anxiety was through the damn roof! It was worse when we had matches or tournaments. All that time, I never told anyone how I felt. I felt like an elephant was sitting on my chest. Sometimes I felt like I was going to pass out. I had no idea what was wrong with me. I had no idea what anxiety was or what the symptoms were. I just thought, *Shut up and just deal with it.* I had this feeling all through high school. I was trying to deal with it, especially when you're too afraid to tell anyone. My brother, on the other hand, was the exact opposite. He took wrestling and football very seriously. He and my dad loved everything about that sport. Nothing bothered them. Now I call them "normies," meaning they are normal people. They don't suffer from addiction or anxiety like I do. I wasn't the best in high school sports, but I was good at throwing a house party.

My first beer with my dad was during my freshman year of high school at our neighbor's house. They had a keg of Labatt Blue. We were only going to show up to say hi. Our house was getting remodeled, so we were staying with my grandparents. I was allowed one beer, but I talked him into three cups. I was putting them down quick. They were tasting really good that night. Honestly, I wanted to stay and drink way more, but my father said no. I was not happy. I wanted to get drunk with everyone else. I loved that feeling of getting drunk. And I thought it was really cool to do. If I wasn't drinking with friends or by myself in high school, I always felt shy and different, then followed by anxiety. Like I said before, I never told anyone the truth about how I really felt; I was just a good actor. I wanted to be that strong person! Men don't have problems or need psychiatrists or counselors. My family just "bulls" our way through the pain. And I was known for not feeling pain and being strong. But damn, did it suck. Also, I had dyslexia; it's a learning disability. Instead of being in classes with all my friends since the first grade, by the seventh grade, I got tested and put in smaller classes, although they were easier, with barely any homework! Bingo! I found my way out of high school. Now I could party.

Chapter 2

Feeling Different Than Others

My whole life, I have felt different. But I didn't notice that until my later ages. Even though I had lots of friends, on the inside, I never had confidence. No matter what I achieved growing up. I always was afraid to speak up for myself. On the other hand, my father never had that issue, but I sure as hell did! I would let people walk all over me, and that got old quick. But like I said, I could never stand up for myself. My inner thoughts would always be, *I'm too stupid, I'm too short, I have a weird body shape*. I always wanted to be six feet tall, but that clearly never happened. But I won't bother you with that.

I just never thought I could measure up. I was always thinking this stupid stuff. I never could walk up to the hottest girl in the room because I knew I would get shut down. I never could handle rejection. Just the thought of it made me worry all day long. And I knew I wasn't the best-looking guy in town, so I made up for it by being funny, crazy, and outgoing. If I didn't have the looks, by god, I was going to make up for it by making you laugh. Also, I was always too nice; you could say I was a people pleaser. But when I got drinking, all that changed. All these worries I listed melted away.

By high school, I was having parties, and I thought I was the life of the party, of course, with the help of beer and whiskey. My friends would use my dad's garage. We would go all night, playing beer pong. Our goal was to get wasted, well, at least mine was. Once I got drunk, I felt invincible. I could talk to anyone, felt six feet tall, and had confidence. I wasn't the fastest drinker, nor could I drink twenty beers, but I sure could get drunk, and that's all I cared about. It wasn't every weekend, but we tried to do it as much as we could. We'd find someone to get beer, sometimes weed, and go all night until the beer was gone.

I was able to socialize and just relax. It turned my brain off to just be like everyone else and laugh. I would get drunk then take a weed break. To me, they went hand in hand. But I started to notice I couldn't outdrink my friends, but I could smoke way more. But the problem was my weed high never lasted as long as my friends did. I would have to smoke way more than everyone else did. But I got to the point where I'd rather smoke weed than drink beer. But I didn't make that switch until college days. By now, high school was winding down, and it was time to graduate. I had no plans afterward. In my town, you either got lucky and went to college, or you went to work at the mines, aboveground or under. Some went to the military just to get away. I was working for my relatives' asphalt company. I worked at the plant where they did the mixture to make the product. I had no plans on leaving or going to college. I would work twelve hours a day, then go through the drive-through and get beer. I could grow a beard, so they thought I was old enough. I was nineteen at the time, I believe. Alcohol and weed always de-stressed my inner thoughts and made me feel normal.

Chapter 3

My First College

One day at work, hungover from the weekend, I was taking a much-needed break and lit up a little joint behind the port-o-johns when I got a phone call from one of my friends. He said, "Hey bro, want to go to community college with me?"

Of course, I was thinking, *Hell no!* Hell, I barely passed high school, and I hated school in general. I was fine staying home and working twelve- to fourteen-hour days in the hot sun, sweating my buns off. I liked lacing my work boots up at the crack of dawn, getting dirty, and working hard for my money. But I thought, *Hell, why not? What's the worst thing that could happen? I'll give it the old college try.*

Community college wasn't as bad as I thought. It was a small campus, and I knew some of the people who went there. I was undecided as a major, so I just took some of the basic classes. I never told a soul about my learning disability because I was afraid I'd get made fun of. So I was treated like everyone else.

That meant I was being taught at the same pace as all my classmates. I wasn't used to that, so you guessed it, my anxiety was creeping back! And I'm awful at taking tests. That's a big part of your grade. I literally thought this was the end of my college career.

As I was coming to take the final exam that morning, I noticed my friend sitting alone on the bench. No one was on that floor. Everyone else in the class was downstairs shooting pool or eating breakfast to get ready for the final. She knew I never ate breakfast, so we just started talking about the test. She asked if I was ready for it. Even though I did study, I told her no. She could see I was starting to sweat and ready to pass out. I could tell she felt bad for me. She knew I had no confidence at all. And I was probably five minutes away from losing my mind and running out the doors and saying, "To hell with this college stuff! I just can't do it! I'm not smart enough. Everyone else can calm down and relax. I can't!"

She tried to calm me down and assure me that everything would be okay. "We both studied for this, and there's no reason why you won't get a passing grade."

As it got closer to test time, my heart pounded out of my chest. She was all calm, cool, and collected. I remember thinking, *God! Why do I have to feel like this? Why can't I just be normal like her?* I had no idea what was to happen next.

Chapter 4

The Day My Whole Life Changed

We had a few minutes left to kill, and I was having a panic attack. She asked me if I had ever heard of Vicodin painkillers. Of course, I'd never been around that kind of stuff until that moment. I was just into drinks and smoked weed. My parents never had that stuff in the house. My parents were what I called normal people. They occasionally drank once in a while, but that's it.

She told me, "It's a painkiller, but also people use it to get high. For some people, it will completely relax them. For others, it does nothing but make them sick. She said, "Take it and see if it helps your anxiety. Swallow it before class and see if you like it."

I took that white pill from her hand and swallowed it. As I walked into class, I felt this warm sensation cover my whole body. I felt lighter—a huge dopamine rush! I had a lot of energy. I was in an amazing mood. I almost forgot about the test. I was talking up a storm. My anxiety and depression were long gone. This was the best I'd felt in a very long time. I couldn't believe it! This was the Ty Howell I'd been searching for! I can remember thinking I never want this feeling to go away!

As I made it to my seat, I was confident for my test. Hell, I was even telling jokes and making people laugh. And I loved doing that. The whole class flew by. I took that test like I studied all week. I was in love with this new me. After I finished the test, I felt confident that I got a passing grade. It was a confidence I had never felt before. After the test, a bunch of us went downstairs to get food and talk. I grabbed my friend to the side and asked for more. She said, "Easy with that stuff. You can get dependent on it."

But the truth was, I was already hooked on it. I just didn't know it yet. But I said, "First off, don't worry about me getting hooked on this. It won't happen to me. I'm not going to do it every day, I promise." Famous last words, right?

The high lasted about four to five hours, if I remember right. And those hours were the best times of my life. In anything I did—watching movies, going to the mall, hanging out with friends—it made me sociable. I could be in large crowds, or I could just go home and relax. I would even ride my Harley high on Vicodin. I loved it! But after the high would wear off, it was back to the old me, which I wasn't happy with. When my high wore off, I would get in a bad mood or just sleep.

The next day, I came back to see my friend to see if I could get more. I'm pretty sure she would not get me anymore. I was upset. My brain wouldn't shut up about taking no for an answer. I started snooping around, and I heard through the grapevine that this other person may have some.

This was a long time ago, so bear with me on my memory. I killed way too many brain cells over my lifetime. But I assure you, this is the true story of my life. Some people are amazed I'm still alive to tell it. Okay, off subject like always. I start talking to this other girl to see what I can find.

Somehow, I found out this person did have what I am looking for. But this time, I had to pay. We finally reached an agreement, and now I was getting more than one. Also, I was already starting to take more than one. But at this stage in my life, I was not remotely thinking about taking more than one or doing it every day. I was just excited I found my own dealer! A whole new world opened up to me. I was basically getting these whenever I want. But now, I was paying for them, and the only money I had was the money I saved up over the summer from working.

Now I was calling this girl up all the time, and for an addict with an endless supply, it was not a good thing. But I had no idea what an addict was or how you became one. Like I said before, I didn't grow up in that world. All I knew was I was having an amazing time with these pills. But now, my tolerance was going up; I was taking more and more. And that's something I never planned for. As soon as my friends were doing three at a time, I was doing ten or more.

Chapter 5

Imaginary Line Crossed?

By that time, all I was thinking about was getting high. It had consumed my brain. It felt like I was calling this person all the time, trying to score. It never dawned on me how much I depended on this. My dealer lived a good distance away from me, but when we were not at college, I would find a way to sneak out to meet her.

If I didn't have enough money, I would use my mom's debit card and get money out of the ATM machine. Or I would take my brother's games and try to sell them for extra cash. As soon as I got enough money, I would leave the house. Sometimes we met at her bedroom window to make the deal. I was over there so much, sometimes early in the morning, because we didn't want her parents to start wondering what was going on. As soon as I got the magical pills, I couldn't wait! I would get a prehigh just thinking about getting high. I'd take them immediately! There was no waiting around with me. By the time I got home, I was feeling amazing again. It turned a boring day into an awesome day. It's a feeling you almost can't describe. It's like your whole body is completely melting into a couch. To this day, I still remember how it feels. I had some of the best times getting high. Nothing mattered during those days. I just was chasing that high.

But as I started with one pill, it was taking me more and more to get high, so I took a step up! I get introduced to a little pill called OxyContin. And wow, these were even better! And you could snort them. And that's exactly what I did. Now at that time, I was about two years into this community college, and that was all they offered at that time. During those college days, I spent a lot of time at Kent State University. I had two friends who went there. And you guessed it, we would party.

So now I applied for the transfer and got accepted. And my short-lived time there was a blur for me. I was hanging out with a frat group, partying almost every weekend, smoking great weed, and snorting anything I could get my hands on. And it was easier to find. I barely went to class. I just smoked weed and snorted pills almost every day.

I was finding new dealers and meeting new friends. It was an amazing time. You could have made a movie of my short time lived there. We lived off campus in a double-wide, my two friends and I.

So now I was getting to know new people, and these people knew some serious dealers. One dealer, more importantly, lived close to my hometown. And he sold everything. He was one of the biggest drug dealers in Ohio. I was crazy enough to want his number, but his good friend that I knew said that it wouldn't be a great idea.

During one night of partying, my buddy and I got so loaded with pain pills I almost overdosed in my own bathroom. We used to have the video, but it's gone by now. But in the middle of getting loaded, I managed to talk my buddy into meeting this dealer the next time we were both home. But I was warned not to beg for his number because it would never happen; he would never deal with me directly. He was not like that. He had trust issues. That was how he got to be as big of a dealer as he was.

The day of the meeting, we drove to this guy's house. I would lie if I told you I wasn't a little nervous. We knocked; he opened the door, gave my friend a hug, then looked me up and down. I thought my life was in danger because I knew he had a gun. Finally, he let me in. As he was crushing up some Oxys, he was asking me some questions. He must have liked me because he offered my friend and me a couple of free pills.

I said, "You don't have to ask me twice!"

He started laughing. We stayed for a bit, and he gave me his number! I was in! As we were heading home, I was told I was lucky. He never usually did that.

That was the day I became friends with one of the biggest dealers I have ever met. No more middleman or other small dealers running out on me. I was finally in control. But my drug habit was out of control. I didn't know it at the time, but I had crossed that imaginary line. And there was no going back now.

I was going to this guy's house all the time now. I would call him up, make sure he had what I needed, and make the drive to pick up my stash. I would make sure I bought enough to get me through a couple of days, but my tolerance had skyrocketed. And there was no end in sight.

One weekend, coming home from college to spend some time with my family, I decided to hit my dealer up for some Oxys. Of course, he had a lot, enough to get me through the weekend. I take the long way home to get the Oxys first, then head home. But as I walk in the door, my family had other plans for me. They must have noticed all the money being spent and my weird behavior. I tried to talk my way out of it. But they were worried and determined! I knew my gig was up, at least for a little while. I wasn't ready to completely quit yet.

I wasn't nervous. I think maybe just upset that I had a ton of pills I couldn't take that weekend. I took the urine test and told them the truth—that I'd been taking painkillers at Kent. I didn't tell them my habit started way back at the community college. Just a little lie. When the test was done, almost every drug came up on it! Damn! Even I was shocked. But hell, I was taking anything I could find. My family was not happy. We all were reading the directions to see if we did it right. Mom was crying, Dad was pissed, and my brother and his girlfriend were shocked; they wouldn't even talk to me. Not a good weekend.

To make things even worse, they tried to do an intervention with me. The rules were simple: rehab or I'd have to start coming home every weekend so they could keep their eyes on me. Of course, I chose to stay home until I got clean and could pass a drug test. But the fact was, none of us knew the severity of my drug problem. Not even me. After a few weekends of passing my drug test, everyone thought I was in the clear. But to me, it was just a break. After I gained their trust back and played by their rules, I was back to seeing my drug dealer. But I remember I was getting tired of the big college scene. I was failing anyway. I wanted to go where my brother was, West Liberty. After taking a bunch of pills to make my anxiety go away, I told my parents my plan. To my surprise, they thought it was a good idea. I had some really fun times at Kent.

My twenty-second birthday, for instance. Story time: All my friends were coming to Kent. I was home getting some goodies for the party. We were in the middle of a huge snowstorm. My brother was the driver, and we were with our best friend, who was a lot younger than us but lived on our street. We'd corrupted him over the years. We somehow make it to my dealer's house to get my stash. They didn't want any of it, but I wasn't going to share anyway. We were now on our way to Kent. As my brother was trying to navigate through the snowstorm, our buddy was in the back with me helping me crush up the Oxys. I was getting torqued. By the time I got up there, I was completely faded! Plus, I was drinking and smoking. I passed out a few times and woke back up. I might have punched a few holes in my room. I was a complete mess, and the party was insane! Now it was time to move everything back home and get ready for West Liberty.

Chapter 6

I Don't Feel in Control Anymore

I got accepted into West Lib. My brother, two friends, and I all lived together in an apartment building. I remember my first weekend, my brother's friend must have been on some crazy stuff because he was all over the place, puking and not making any sense. I knew these were my people. They were crazy and having a good time. I fit right in. Now instead of doing pills 24-7, I switched to weed. It was easier to get. But I still did my fair share of pills. I was in a smaller college, but we still had a great time. We didn't go out much. We had one close-knit group of friends we all smoked with. Only three of us did pills. My brother stayed away. He tried one night at a party. I forget what I gave him. I was having the time of my life as always, and we split up. Someone tracked me down and said, "Your brother is really sick. You need to go see him."

As I found my brother, he was sweating really bad and lying on a bed. He looked like death. Everyone was worried. I told him he would be fine and left. But that's what drugs do to an addict. You only care about yourself and your next high. I was an awful person. At this point, nothing had changed for me. I was still doing pills, smoking weed, and drinking. But at no point did I ever think I had a problem. Maybe because I stayed in a constant high. Sometimes I would notice my friends would take a break for a couple of days, but I couldn't. I needed my painkillers. My grades were good but not good enough to stay at college. Same with my brother. Once again, I chose feeding my addiction instead of going to class. After two long years of good ole West Lib, we decided to quit, go back home, and get full-time jobs. I called my faithful drug dealer to tell the news. Of course, he was just as thrilled as I was. So we packed up everything and came home for good.

We both got jobs at an asphalt plant, making good money. And yes, you guessed it, I was back to pills full time again. My brother and I worked for two years at that company. During that time, my parents caught me abusing painkillers and smoking weed a lot. Hell, I would even do it with the guy I worked with. I think my family and I thought rehab was a serious need for me at this point. But we lived in a small town where everyone knew everyone, and the whole town knew my family.

It seemed like the whole town had great respect for my parents and grandparents. My grandpa was a self-made man who started his own company. He employed lots of people and installed two-way radios in police cars and such. He did very well for himself and retired early. I didn't want my business being leaked out and be the talk of the town. That would devastate my family. For a long time, I was drinking, taking pills, and now I was smoking synthetic weed so I would pass my parents' drug tests.

I wasn't worried about all the painkillers. I knew it would only stay in my system for at the most three to four days. It didn't matter if I was at work or at home. I was getting high pretty much every day. I pretty much had to. At this point, I was a slave to it. But of course, I loved it too. It was my first love. But in the process of my drug addiction, I lost all my friends and girlfriends because I chose the drugs over them. If my addiction called, I answered, no matter what. Nothing was getting in my way either.

At this point in my life, all my friends and my brother were starting to settle down, getting married and having kids. I had a girl-friend, but my drug addiction was more important. I obsessed over it. It took over my brain. So they wouldn't stick around long. And when we would break up, I would blame it on them. It was never my fault. I didn't have a problem; they did. And everyone believed me, even my parents. My parents knew something was wrong with me, but what could they do about it? I had to want to get help; they couldn't force me. They worried 24-7.

We were on nights shift, driving these huge rock trucks. During our break, my coworker mentioned he had some on him. I thought about it for a minute. I knew the right choice was to tell him no, but like I said, I was a full-blown drug addict. I didn't have a say in the matter. I wasn't in control anymore. I told him, "Of course I'll take some!" And *bam!* That amazing feeling found its way back to me again. I was back on cloud nine once again. I was only going to do it that one night, then never again. *I can do this. I just have to try harder!* Once the high wore off, my brain said, "You still have your drug dealer." I needed that feeling every day. Now I was back to buying them by the dozen. Taking twenty-five to thirty at a time twice a day. And I was left thinking, *How did I get here? What am I doing?*

I couldn't believe I was taking as many as I am. Like I said, twenty-five to thirty pills twice a day! And above all else, I could function like a normal person sober. People who knew how many I did at a time thought I was crazy or had a death wish. But this was normal to me. If I didn't take that many, I didn't get as high. And that was a waste to me.

To be honest, I myself didn't know how I was still alive. Up to that point, I'd never overdosed. So here I was at this new job, getting high like I said I wouldn't do. I got that obsession back in my mind. And I had money to pay for it. No more stealing off my mom or taking pills from my grandma and when she noticed, blaming it on her caretaker. Like I said before, I wasn't a good person.

After six or seven months into the mine, our pit got shut down. I got laid off and started collecting unemployment money, which wasn't much. So now I was sweating it because where was I going to get the money to pay for my habit?

Chapter 7

Getting Worse

By now I had lost all my friends. I was living with my parents because all my hard-earned money had gone to drugs for a very long time now. And oh yes, I was jobless! But you guessed it, still not hit my rock bottom. I guess I still needed to go through more misery to figure it out. By now, my brother had a serious girlfriend, and they had a daughter now. Yes, I was an uncle. I was pretty much the last one left of all my friends to not be married or have my own family. Yes, that bothered me, but I didn't have a choice. Being a drug addict was far way more important. I wasn't allowed to think of anything else. If the drugs called, I had to answer—drop everything I was doing and answer! Hell of a life, I know.

I had a girlfriend at that time. I wasn't sure if she knew about my drug problem or not. It wouldn't stop me even if she did, though. I never told her, but you could always tell if I was or not. Sometimes I'd be talking to her and pass out or nod off, then wake back up real quick. And I was somewhat shady at times. We dated for a good while. We lived with my parents for a while in the basement. My brother and his wife lived there as well. We had a full house plus a baby. I ended up getting a job that I was excited about and started that in 2014. So you can say I'd been battling addiction for a very long time now, and still, I was too proud to ask for help. I knew there was a stigma against drug addicts, and I didn't want to admit I was one or needed help! So now I had a good job, a possible career. And

I like the people I worked with. Basically, a wild bunch of people. So I fit right in once again. My girlfriend and I still lived with my parents and now started the conversation of moving out. I really didn't want to. A house mortgage would interfere with my drug habit. We couldn't have that now, could we?

So back to my new job. My first day of training, I met two important people in my life that would affect me later in my life story. I was getting trained by them. It was twelve-hour shifts, so we spent a lot of time together. Every day I talked to this guy, we had more and more in common. The other guy just listened and laughed, but me and the other guy were stubborn and bullheaded. He also had an addiction. That fascinated me. Plus, he got clean and stayed clean still to that day. Over twelve years. He did it through a program called AA. At that time in my life, I still wasn't ready to tell him the truth about what I was going through, but I had a feeling he could see right through my pain.

As I said about my last job, I was going to try and get clean. I wanted to treat this new job the same way—a new beginning, a new Ty! I was getting older now, and I didn't know how much longer I could live like this. My lifestyle was out of control! My girlfriend and I decided to move out and found a small house close to where I worked. We even got engaged in the process. But of course, you can find drugs anywhere you go if you're looking and asking. But I was still sober for now. A few weeks went by, and I started getting that itch again. I ended up breaking down and found the right person to ask. He directed me to someone who never ran out! So for the hundredth time, I started back to using. To make matters worse, I didn't live far from this guy. But back then, I didn't see it that way. I was out of my parents' home, I had a drug dealer within walking distance, and I was close to work!

I was getting pills almost every day, and I was taking a lot of them, twenty-five to thirty at a time. I spent a lot of money on it too. I kept it very hidden from my girlfriend. I would even do them at work; I was a functioning addict. But also every day, I would talk to my sober buddy at work. I would open up more and more every day. This had gone on for some time now. I could tell he was trying to help me, but again I wasn't ready.

If my new dealer ran out, which I was told he wouldn't, but he had no idea how many I was taking. I got introduced to Suboxone. It was cheaper, and Suboxone actually helped you, if taken right and monitored by a clinic and doctor, get off drugs. But anything I took or smoked, I had to have a lot of it, and I did it every day if I could. People thought it was unreal, the amount of substances it took me to get and stay high. I would try pretty much anything and everything.

As years passed, I was still living close to work, still getting high off anything I could find.

The drugs were starting to tear me and my girlfriend apart. But now she was more than my girlfriend; she was my fiancée, and we even had a wedding date planned. But she was finally at the end of her ropes with me. Yes, she'd found out about my addiction and told my parents about me a few times. But like I said, what could they do? They tried everything with me. Nothing worked. We ended up calling off the wedding and going our separate ways. It sent me into a depression. I was doing what I always do—get high.

My sober friend at work started noticing my behavior and kept working his magic on me. My answer was still the same: No! You're not going to take the one thing I love away from me, and the drugs love me back. I stayed single for a while. I dated off and on, nothing too serious. I had moments of sobriety but still couldn't kick it completely. I remember crying in the shower because I was so lost! I even started praying to see if it would help. I isolated myself from my family. I just stayed home and did what I knew how to do best.

Chapter 8

Introduced to Kratom

For what seemed to be the hundredth time, it seemed like I got sober for a while then failed again. It was an up-and-down battle that I was losing. But here I went again at an attempt to do the impossible. I was getting through the withdrawals and starting to feel better. I was still living in my own home, which I kind of let go to shit because I lost interest in doing chores like mowing the grass and other things since I'd rather get high and sleep.

I believe it was around 2018–2019. I'd been battling addiction forever now. I couldn't even remember being sober for a long period of time. I thought maybe I had severe depression or anxiety and just maybe I used drugs to cope with it. But what did I know? I was no therapist. So I went and found one to help me. To my amazement, they couldn't even help or keep me sober.

I was on Facebook, and that night my whole life changed. I fell completely head over heels with this girl from my hometown. We started talking, and I was on cloud nine! As a bonus, she had two kids from a previous marriage. We hit it off really fast. Somehow I knew she was the one for me.

The only thing was, I really wanted to be sober the first time we met. But I was so nervous and didn't want to mess it up that I couldn't help myself. She still met the real me. I just had more confidence because of the painkillers.

After meeting, things started moving pretty quickly. The only thing was, I was still off and on with my sobriety. Now I was on kratom. You can find it in head shops and some gas stations. The kicker is, you can pass a drug test while on it. That was huge for me. I thought I'd found the holy grail of drugs. And if you take enough of it, kratom mimics painkillers.

We went Facebook official within a month or two. It was like heaven on earth. The only thing that could stop us was my drug addiction. I kept it a secret for as long as I could. But I knew she was going to find out soon. When she found out, she was very upset. I told her that was why I was always going home all the time—to get high. I wasn't used to kids or that lifestyle, but I tried my best. I told her I was trying to quit, but she didn't know how bad it really was.

Of course, we had our disagreements and occasional argument here and there, but we loved each other and wanted to work it out. I put that woman through hell and back. And when we would have a big fight, I didn't know how to express myself, so I would run away to my house or my parents' and get high. We had two or three really good years together until things went south. But before all that, we had big plans.

One was to get married in Florida and stay at my grandma's condo. And number 2 was to have a baby together. We thought maybe a child would get me completely sober. As we were trying for a baby, we had some complications. It wasn't as easy as we thought it would be. We tried and tried but nothing. We started planning the wedding. We were both very excited.

Everything was all planned out, and we had our plane tickets bought. The only problem, her kids couldn't go, and we didn't like that idea. A week before our wedding, we had to make the hard decision: get married in Florida or wait till we get home.

It was a hard choice, but we decided to wait and just go to Florida and relax. Sarah would never admit it, but it turned into a vacation from hell. I really wanted to get married there. I was so excited. When we decided to wait, I got depressed, so I found out where to get kratom. And every day, we had to make an hour's drive to get it.

I wasn't in the best moods either. All Sarah wanted to do was go to the pool and see the ocean. We did swim at the pool a lot, but when it was time to spend the day at the ocean, I had to ruin it because I met a dude the night before to set up a deal for a weed vapor pen since I couldn't bring one on the flight down. Trust me, she was thrilled with that one! All in all, it was a really nice vacation with the love of my life, but deep down, I knew I could have made it a lot better for her.

And that's exactly what addiction does to you. You're not in control anymore. As much as you want to be, addiction always wins. Sarah was my everything, but I could feel us drifting apart when we came back home.

Chapter 9

Losing the Battle

When we got back from Florida, I had to go back to work, working night shift. We didn't talk at all for three days straight. I spent those three days numbing my feelings as usual. I knew something was wrong, but I didn't want to acknowledge it. That week of work, I was diving headfirst heavily on kratom and weed.

On the last day of work, I got a phone call at work. I looked, and it was Sarah; she never called me at work. I answered, and she said, "Hey, just to let you know, I missed my period, and I took a pregnancy test. It came back positive."

I was speechless. I said, "So we're having a baby?"

Sarah said, "Yes, we're having a baby."

To be honest, I was terrified and excited at the same time.

So I told her, "Well, this means I need to get completely sober." She knew I was still using, obviously, because of the vacation we just got back from. But she didn't know how severe it really was. And yes, I was honest and filled her in. I told her that rehab might be needed. I told her I needed to call my mom; she might know what to do. I called her up and said, "I have good and bad news." My heart was pounding out of my chest. "Bad news is, I'm still using. And I probably need rehab or professional help." But was I really ready to fully commit?

As you can probably guess, Mom wasn't too happy with me. But deep down, she knew. Now she said, "What's the good news?"

I said, "Sarah and I are having a baby!" Mom was very excited!

We started looking up detox places. We found one close to our hometown. It was in a hospital. I got approved to miss work. I kept it a secret from everyone. Only my family and Sarah knew. It was a seven- to eight-day stay. I was optimistic and nervous at the same time. My mom first took me and Sarah to the baby appointment. I wanted to be there for Sarah to see what her doctors had to say about the upcoming pregnancy. After her appointment, Sarah and I said our goodbyes and said, "See ya in seven days."

Mom dropped me off, and away I went to my first detox. It was me and two other guys. We had our own beds and around-the-clock nurse supervision. We ate horrible hospital food and had a TV we watched. They gave us meds to ease the pain of the withdrawals. Plus, we would see the doctor once a day to see how we were doing.

The place was no Taj Mahal by any means, but it was okay. There wasn't much to do but watch TV, walk around in circles, which I did a lot of.

After I spent my eight days there, I got cleared to leave. But I remember feeling I wasn't sure if I was ready to leave. I remember staying sober for a week. I remembered I had a weed vapor pen in my vehicle. They never searched our cars! Temptation was calling me hard! I tried to resist, but my addiction was much too powerful for me to handle. And just like that, I was back to my old behaviors yet again.

I still had time off work, so I even started back with the kratom as hard as I could. My addiction was skyrocketing once again. I didn't tell anyone I relapsed yet. I was too embarrassed to do that. After doing much soul-searching, I knew I had to do something. I contacted my sober working buddy. He said, "If you turn yourself into the company, they will get you professional help." That was scary for me to do. After keeping it a secret for all this time, now I'm turning myself in? I didn't want anyone knowing my personal business. Finally, I gave in and set up a meeting with the HR lady.

I went into that meeting absolutely terrified! I told my work the truth: "I'm a functioning drug addict. I have been for a very long time. And I need help."

To my surprise, they told me to take as much time as I needed. Oh, how could I forget? I also told them, "I'm going to be a first-time dad as well." I left that meeting breathing again! I got to keep my job and attempted to get clean. As soon as I got to my place, I started doing research. I thought detox and residential were the same thing. I had no idea they were different, separate programs. Detox was allowing your body to rest and get the poison out of your body. The residential program was four weeks long or longer. You discover what makes you use and get a clear meaning of the word *addiction*. Usually, you have classes, counselors, therapists, doctors, and psychiatrists you see almost every day. Plus, you're in with a bunch of other addicts, so you form a bond with them. Residential is an awesome program.

So anyways, I started calling places in Ohio, California, Florida. They all seemed good, but I didn't want to go too far because of Sarah being pregnant, and sick all the time. So I made the choice to head to Tennessee, a place called Cornerstone. It had the best rating. I called them and answered a few questions. They accepted my insurance. They wanted me quickly. Before I went to rehab, I decided to go stay with Sarah at the hospital. She was really sick. I wanted to see her before I left for a month. Yes, the stay at Cornerstone was four weeks to complete the full program. And for how sick I was, I needed every bit of that month. Yes, I was still using. It was to the point where I had to use to function and not be sick. I really wasn't using to get high anymore. I was doing it so I wouldn't get sick. I was able to see Sarah a few days before I had to go home and pack. It was an eight-hour drive to Cornerstone. I stayed up all night getting high and got a late start and missed my scheduled intake time, where they start the process of getting you in the computer and ready for detox. I had to get a hotel for the night and check in the next day. At the hotel, I had one last go at it. It was just me, but I could always entertain myself when I was using. I was just enjoying my last night of freedom before the work started. I took enough kratom pills to kill a normal person and smoked my favorite weed. I was starting to feel really dizzy from all the kratom pills. I must have taken fifty pills at once. I'd only been close to overdosing a few times, and I was starting to think I made a mistake on how many I had taken.

But I was a seasoned vet! I knew I could shake this feeling off. It wasn't working. I started fading in and out of consciousness. I decided to get out of bed and eat my leftovers from what I ordered. As soon as I get up, I was seeing double of everything in my room. I barely managed to get a shower. I was still faded. I ended up passing out.

Chapter 10

Rehab

I woke up the next morning with a huge headache. I had no recollection of what had happened last night. I was still somewhat out of it when I woke up. I noticed I had slept in and missed my intake again. I had to call them to make sure they would still take me in that day. I guess they're used to that insane behavior, so they told me to just come in when I was ready.

I forgot to bring a lot of items I was told to bring, but I showed up anyway. The place was huge, and I already didn't like it. As I was sitting in my car in the parking lot, a thought popped into my brain to go get some kratom and head home. This rehab stuff wasn't for me. I started thinking about Sarah, my family, and our unborn child. I took a deep breath, grabbed my clothes, and took one last rip out of my weed pen. I started my walk to the building to get checked in.

Everyone was really nice. Made you feel right at home. I was staying for the whole thirty days. It was a week or so of detox treatment, where they monitored you closely around the clock and kept your withdrawals in check. That pretty much meant they made sure you were as comfortable as you could be. Withdrawals can be the worst thing in the world to go through. Detox was simple. You just relaxed and watched TV. They had a patio you could go outside and smoke cigs. You were well fed. I spent seven days in detox. By the way, withdrawal symptoms, for those of you who never felt it, are hot and cold flashes, extreme sweats, and lack of energy or wanting to do

28

anything. You feel nauseated all the time, you're tired 24-7, and you can't eat or sleep. It's awful!

I managed to get through detox. I also made lots of cool friends. You did everything together with these people. Once you reached the residency program, you had more freedom. You could call your family, which I did almost every day. I got to call Sarah as well. She was starting to feel better. In residential, you had classes all day every day. You discover you had a sickness—and yes, it is a disease and also hereditary. If your addiction goes untreated for a long time, chances are you may never get sober for good. It's a lifelong disease, and it can be fatal. It's also progressive, which means it will continue to grow worse with time as brain changes continue to affect thought, behavior patterns, and compulsive use.

After thirty-one days, I did the unthinkable! I graduated rehab and got my thirty-day coin. I was heading home a new man. Nothing could stop me now. I called Sarah and told her the good news. I managed to get to her house around midnight. Hell, I even lost weight.

I was ready to take on the world! I got to Sarah's house. I was so happy to see her. She even had a little baby bump. I was so excited for our life together. I waited a month and called my sober buddy from work, who first trained me at work. He was the first person outside my family I contacted. I told him I just got out of a thirty-day rehab. And I needed a sponsor. He shockingly said he didn't sponsor, but he would help me on my journey. I started doing AA with him, and we became closer.

Months and months went by, and I was still going strong. I couldn't believe it! I was finally doing it with the help of my family, Sarah, her family, and my sponsor. I was making meetings, collecting chips or monthly sobriety coins. I got to six months, and I started thinking about my one-year anniversary. I talked it over with my sponsor. He said I was letting my ego run wild. And that was a very bad thing.

I politely disagreed with him, not even seeing he might have a point. I was on the Vivitrol shot; I started it at Cornerstone to give myself a better chance of staying clean. It's a monthly shot given by your hometown nurse practitioner. It helps fight cravings, and it keeps you from getting high. So if you were to mess up and take a few pills, the shot would block you from feeling good.

Coming up on month number 7, I was working nights and had an appointment to get my shot the morning I finished up. Even though it was in the morning, I was confident I would be able to make it. Then I had to work that night.

I ended up sleeping in that day and missed my shot. I got up in enough time to make it to work on time. I thought to myself, *I can't believe I just missed my shot!* Now I was starting to panic a little bit. I was now on my way to work, thinking about getting some kratom. Instead of calling my sponsor, I drove to the gas station and got a bag. I looked at the pills for a few minutes, and just like that, my sobriety was over! I thought to myself as I grabbed the first pill out of the forty-nine left I was going to swallow, *Is there any faith left that I will get completely sober? Or will I die like this?*

Chapter 11

It's Now or Never!

Now that I was back to using again, I kept it a secret from everyone, even my sponsor. Months went by, and I was back to using every day like I said I wouldn't. I always thought to myself, *Just one bag, Ty. What could it hurt? You can control it.* My daughter was born, and I couldn't have been any happier. We named her Hayden. And yes, I was still in active addiction. I was too ashamed to say anything because rehab couldn't even save me. And it was the best one in the nation! I was living with my parents but staying with Sarah most of the time.

It seemed like every week, my mom was finding kratom bags now. I was high even with my daughter around. Everyone thought having a baby would change me, but it just made my anxiety worse. I would tell Sarah I was sober. Whether she believed me or not, I didn't have a clue. I just didn't want her taking Hayden away from me. My mom, at this point, was the only person who knew I'd relapsed. I even lied to my sponsor. Also, I could tell Sarah's and my relationship was getting rocky again. That added extra depression and anxiety.

Finally, after months and months of being lost and not knowing what to do, my mom and I were in the basement. She said, "I found a couple of bags of kratom under your dresser." For some reason, I wasn't worried about being caught for the thousandth time. Either I was just used to it by now, or maybe it was a weight lifted off my shoulders. All these years of craziness, running around to get it and lying, maybe I was finally ready to quit. I was getting older, and I was not sure how much my body would hold up.

After Mom confronted me that day, I didn't say anything; I just remember agreeing with her. I told her I was ready this time. I had two weeks of vacations left. As soon as my mom and I talked about another visit to rehab, I started calling around. This time, I wanted to stay in Ohio. I'd heard about this place called ORAC; it's a small thirty-day detox and residential program located in Columbus, Ohio. I called them up and got accepted right away. I told them I was in active use with kratom, and I couldn't stop. By the way, kratom is legal, but it's still very addictive! I couldn't stop no matter how hard I tried!

Kratom was my real hell! It took everything away from me. My family, I felt like this was my last chance to prove to them I can do this. Even Sarah was getting fed up with me. I barely saw my daughter. I felt like I was stuck in hell with kratom and there was nothing I could do! ORAC was my last chance. I had to wait four days, then I was on vacation for twenty-four days. The only way I could get through those four days without feeling like death was, yes, you guessed it, kratom. Those four days felt like forever. Finally, day number 4! I headed down to rehab, got checked in, and realized this rehab was much different. It was smaller and tailored to you. It was more personalized.

I loved that. That meant more time with my counselor and therapist. I learned a lot more about myself and addiction. I also made a lot of friends and successfully completed my second rehab. I called my family and told them I made a breakthrough here. Sarah and I talked every day as well. I also told her I felt like a new person. I'd made a lot of progress in the last thirty days. She was just as excited as I was. I was coming home. But again, I had to add, was I really ready to go home and dive into the real world, or should I have tried sober living like they told me I should? So for a few months, I slowly got adjusted to a different life of being sober. Remember, I was diagnosed as a severe addict. I had demons I was trying to chase away. But of course, I told them no sober living; I'd try IOP this time. IOPs or intensive outpatient was basically going to more classes about addiction.

A couple of days before leaving, that was the exact choice I made. It was closer to home. And you stayed home, not at rehab. In IOPs, you still got drug tested, and it lasted six months or more.

I didn't have any traditional IOP classes near me, so I got hooked up with a program called AWARE. Same concept but they came to you. Zoom calls and a counselor came to your home and talked to you for an hour, plus drug test. I loved this program. Plus, they had therapists, nurse practitioners. Anything you need they would do for you.

After a month of being home from ORAC and doing the AWARE program, I failed miserably! God, what was it going to take for me to get this? But a lot of stuff was going on in my life that I couldn't handle. Sarah and I didn't work out, and I didn't take it very well. I told my sponsor, but he wasn't mad. He had a feeling that this was going to happen. He always told me till I let go completely and accept God, I would continue to be miserable.

I finally worked up enough courage and told my AWARE group I used again. Instead of dropping me like they should have, we started thinking outside the box. We talked micro-dosing down, Vivitrol shot, rehab for the fourth time, and Suboxone clinic. I'd abused Suboxone before but never tried to get sober with it.

I knew there was a stigma against it. We had a group meeting. We decided to go for it and find a clinic. I started doing research online and found a clinic thirty minutes away.

I called up BrightView, and they seemed really professional. I went in for my first appointment. It lasted about four hours. I even got my own therapist. We got along great, and I could fully open up to her. This place did things right and really cared about you.

They started you out at a low dose and monitored you from there. The only scary thing was, I had to really respect this medicine this time, or I would be back to square one again. With the help of my family, BrightView, and AWARE, I stuck to the plan, of course, being drug-tested by AWARE and BrightView. I started picking up momentum. Days turned into weeks, and weeks turned into months.

I am now over five months clean. Happy and enjoying life sober, finally. So even though stigmas can discourage you, don't listen to the noise. It's saving my life. I am even seeing my daughter on my days off work. Hayden and I have a wonderful relationship.

Chapter 12

Life in Recovery

Life so far has been great. I never thought I'd be alive to tell this story or sober. Many people wrote me off as a lost cause, and maybe I was. I am living proof that you can recover from addiction. I've been through hell and back, and to be honest, this was the hardest thing I've ever done in my life.

But the thing is, this battle isn't over and will never be. It's a constant struggle to stay clean. You have to surround yourself with positive people. I go to AA meetings and have the same sponsor that helps me out a lot. You also have to have the tools to use in case you have a bad day and want to use. Today, I feel like I have the tools to use; life still isn't perfect. I still get put in situations, but I don't have to get high to escape it. I hope my story will touch someone's heart and mind and give them the strength to make that call and get help. It just takes one call, and your phone isn't that heavy to pick up and dial. If I can do it, anyone can. Addiction doesn't discriminate. It affects everyone and takes everything. My name is Ty Howell. And this was my story.

Thank you for reading!

About the Author

Ty Howell lives in a small town and has a beautiful daughter. He grew up in a loving family. He had close friends, and they all did things together. Never did he think this would happen to him. He did not want to become an addict. He tried to hide it from his family and friends. However, it catches up with you, and you need help. He has faced many obstacles and setbacks, but he has learned his strength. He would not wish this on anyone, and he hopes that somehow, he or his book could be of help to somebody.

Printed in the USA
CPSIA information can be obtained
at www.ICGtesting.com
CBHW071737230824
13474CB00008B/390